REMINISCING TOGETHER

This book is one in the PRIME TIME™ series from CompCare Publishers. PRIME TIME™ books address a wide range of issues and attitudes related to growing older. They are intended primarily, but not exclusively, for people past midlife—especially for those who are choosing to grow older with courage and imagination.

Other books available in
the PRIME TIME™ series:

A Touch of Sage

Never Too Late

Time to Become Myself

REMINISCING TOGETHER

Ways to Help Us Keep Mentally Fit as We Grow Older

Howard I. Thorsheim, Ph.D.
and Bruce B. Roberts, Ph.D.

CompCare® Publishers

Minneapolis, Minnesota

Library of Congress Cataloging-in-Publication Data
Thorsheim, Howard I.
    Reminiscing together : ways to help us keep mentally fit as we
grow older / by Howard I. Thorsheim and Bruce B. Roberts
        p. cm.
    ISBN 0-89638-221-4
    1. Reminiscing in old age. 2. Memory. I. Roberts, Bruce B. II.
Title.
BF724.85.R45T46 1990
155.67—dc20   90-2043
                                                                  CIP

Cover and interior design by MacLean & Tuminelly
Cover illustration by Dan Woychick

Inquiries, orders, and catalog requests should be addressed to
CompCare Publishers
2415 Annapolis Lane
Minneapolis, Minnesota 55441
Call toll free 800/328-3330
(Minnesota residents 612/559-4800)

5	4	3	2	1
94	93	92	91	90

Contents

Acknowledgments

We'd like to express our thanks to the several
hundred people from the Ebenezer Society
Learning Opportunities program and the St. Olaf
Elderhostel programs, who participated in our
course "Memories of Your Own Life Experiences"
and who suggested that this book be written.

Our special appreciation also goes to the
members of the initial Ebenezer Society planning
group who helped us as consultants, suggesting
directions this book should take to be useful:
Olive Berget, Henrietta Gronlid, Fernanda
Malmin, Florence Martin, Martha Mattson,
Margaret Nodolf, Mildred Sebo, Madeline
Thompson, and James Loken-Egdahl. Thanks
also to Lydia Quanbeck, director of continuing
education at St. Olaf College, for her empowering
leadership; to Kate Towle, editor, for her
thoughtful and patient editing of this manuscript;
to David Roberts for his helpful stories; to Steve
Roberts for listening to Edna Solberg's story of her
early days at Bethel Lutheran Church in
Northfield, Minnesota; and to all those who
participated in our program "Elders As
Consultants: The Lifestories Program." Special

thanks to Clara Berg and all of her enthusiastic friends at Red Oak Grove Lutheran Church in Blooming Prairie, Minnesota.

The special contributions of Lawrence Bunde, Leslie Gustafson, Elmer Hjortland, Borghild Loken, Kathy Nelson, Omar Otterness, Dorothy Peters, Lois Rand, and Gladys Thorsheim are acknowledged with great appreciation.

We would also like to express our appreciation for the grant from the Minnesota Private College Research Foundation with funds from the Blandin Foundation of Minnesota for support of "Elders as Consultants: The Lifestories Program," through which production and distribution of the original edition of this book was made possible. Special thanks are due to Chandra Mehrotra for his encouragement of our work and his perceptive and helpful observations, and Amy Carroll and Jane Greathouse for their significant help on this project.

We also thank Loraine DiPietro, director of the National Information Center on Deafness, for her help in reviewing material in Chapter 7, "Being Honest about Limitations"; Jamie Casabianca Hilton, American Foundation for the Blind national consultant on aging; Philip Wong-Cross of the Library of Congress National Library Service for the Blind and Physically Handicapped for his help with resources cited in the appendices; and Betty Davis, American

Association of Retired Persons (AARP) program specialist, for her encouragement and support of this book project and her key role in the AARP Reminiscence Program.

Thanks to Julie Thorsheim and Jan Roberts for the special people they are in our lives; and to our children, Peter, Thomas, Kristoffer, and Martin Thorsheim, and Steven, David, and Susan Roberts, for their contributions to new memories and new stories.

We also thank you for reading this book. Your thoughts and suggestions will make the next edition of this book even more useful. We would like to hear from you.

Howard Thorsheim and Bruce Roberts
St. Olaf College
Northfield, Minnesota

Introduction

Why Memory Is Important

Let us share with you a story about one of Howard's experiences with memory:

It was a rather cold and blustery day in the late fall. I was driving home from the college where I teach a course on the psychology of learning and remembering. I needed to pick up some milk from the small grocery store about a block from my home. I stopped, got out of the car, waved to some of my students who were standing outside the store, and went in. I bought the milk, went outside, and headed home. I was surprised at how much colder the weather seemed since I had left the store, but shrugged my shoulders, tucked my chin down into my collar, and headed down the street. As I came up the driveway to our home, I could see my wife, Julie, coming to the door to greet me. It was a friendly sight. As I came up to the door, she asked, "Where's the car?"

"Car?" I replied.

"You had it with you when you left this morning," she answered.

All of a sudden several things became clear to me. That's why it had become so much colder coming from the store than it had been going to the store. I had driven to the store, parked, gone in to buy milk, come out, and walked home, forgetting the car parked in front of the store.

✦

The point is: everybody forgets. Forgetting is a human problem that happens even to college professors like Howard who teach courses in the psychology of learning and remembering. When we forget, we are reminded that we are human.

Forgetting has many causes. Some can be changed. Some cannot. But we all can agree that remembering is important to us. Maybe that's the reason you've begun to read this book.

We asked many people of all ages, including elders, what they wanted a book about memory fitness to include. Here, in their own words, are some of their concerns:

✦

I can't remember names! But my memory for past events is good. It's always been hard for me to remember names—especially when being introduced. It's very embarrassing when, in turn, I do the introductions. I would like to be able to remember names of new acquaintances. I'm finding it harder to think of a name when someone else asks about a person both the asker and I know, or about a place I've been. Also, reading an article and forgetting most of it when I go to discuss it—that's a problem for me. As I get older it seems that I can remember many things in detail that happened early in my life better than the many things of late. My immediate memory seems to depart.

I would like to find out what research shows about the way we remember, and how we can perhaps develop skills, even at this point in our life, to improve our memory and its functioning.

In speaking, I can't think of a word I want to say and I can't think of a substitute word.

Remembering is so important in life—to happiness and living day to day. Why is it so hard to remember small things? Is it concentration that's so hard?

Older persons often seem "expected" to not have adequate memories. If this is inevitable, is there something I can do to help me cope? I would like to have my memory stimulated and developed at a time in life when forgetfulness is a slight but increasing problem.

✦

Just why is it important to remember? As the above comments suggest, our ability to remember helps us make sense of our lives. Each of us has a history of unique personal experiences that makes us who we are. Memory is our ability to store these experiences in our minds. When we use the word memories, we are referring to the thoughts, feelings, and experiences we store and later bring to mind throughout our lives.

Our memory ability helps us adapt to an ever-changing world. This unique ability reminds us of people's names, street addresses, how and when to water our plants, even what recipe to serve to a group of friends. Recalling past experiences, thoughts, and feelings helps us think of ways to be calm and alert when new situations arise.

When, on the other hand, we cannot remember something, we may feel lonely and disorganized. At such times, we need activities to help us strengthen our memory ability. The more actively we try to remember, the more meaningful our experiences become—and the more we can share our life experiences together. That is why an advisory group of elders suggested that we write this book. In this book, we explore four important ways to help our memories work for us:

1. Reminiscing, or sharing memories of life experiences (Chapter 1)

2. Learning how memory works (Chapter 2)

3. Using our senses to stimulate memory (Chapters 3-6)

4. "Pump-priming" activities to strengthen memory (Chapter 8)

Let's talk briefly about each of these.

1. Reminiscing

When we share our life experiences with others, and in turn we listen to theirs, we use our imagination.

The French word "souvenir," or "to remember," has become our word for treasure, or keepsake. Our unique experiences are like precious pictures or other mementos stored in a treasure box. We bring them out from time to time to admire them and the experiences they remind us of. The more we take them out, the more familiar and dear they become to us. If, however, we keep them in their box most of the time, we almost forget that we have them.

To take this idea further—imagine that you have removed a very special picture from your treasure box. What would happen if you shared a story about your picture with a friend? Maybe then that person would, in turn, share with you an experience they had. You may learn from sharing your experience to cherish it all the more. At the same time, you can learn what experiences are cherished by your friend or loved one.

After you have shared what is precious to you, it is likely to become more valuable to you. It also means more to the person you shared it with. Whenever that person sees a picture like yours, she or he will probably remember you.

A memory shared is a bridge that connects your life with someone else's.

When we share our experiences, we get to know ourselves and one another better. And we gain trust in our relationships with loved ones and friends. These bonds with others add meaning to our lives. We are reminded that there is a world to discover outside of our experience—a world that constantly offers new things, places, and people to know. It's a world that stirs memories that surprise and comfort us.

Sharing our experiences with others—we like to call it "storysharing"—is a comfortable way to explore our world in the company of people who are close to us. It brings us closer to more people. Most of all, it brings us back in touch with how very special our own lives are.

2. Learning How Memory Works

Understanding how memory works can help us. We can learn to store information in an organized way. This will not keep us from forgetting, of course. But it will make it easier to remember details.

No one is born with a perfect memory. We will remember some things better than others. How do we use our memory to search for information we know? How do we identify things as familiar? When we learn things "by heart," what, in fact, are we doing? Together, we will explore the facts of memory, the what, when, where, why, and how of remembering.

3. Using Our Senses to Stimulate Memory

We experience our world through our eyes, ears, nose, mouth, and sense of touch. Our senses can be considered as "building blocks" for remembering experiences and ideas. Each moment, we are taking in information about our world through our senses.

Seeing

When we truly see what is around us, we become curious to learn more. Generally, the more time we take to learn about something we see, the more we will remember about it later on.

Our memory helps us to combine mental images of our past with images of things we would like to have happen to us. Some call this thinking, reflecting, or daydreaming.

One of our friends said:

✦

I like to close my eyes and remember a favorite place from my childhood. Memories flood back as I look around with my mind's eye. I see all kinds of things: people, my dog, a favorite plum tree I used to climb (it had a swing hanging from one of its branches), nighthawks swooping and diving through the air after insects.

✦

Hearing

Hearing a familiar voice or listening to a favorite song—like "Down by the Old Mill Stream"—can make us feel wonderful! Why? Because sounds help us recall former moments when perhaps we felt content and hopeful. The memory of favorite sounds brings joy and hope to our present thoughts!

Smelling and Tasting

Memories are often stirred by fragrances we've smelled or by aromas of foods we've tasted. When it comes to reminiscing, fragrances and aromas are especially important. They have a way of bringing us back to emotional memories, or feelings, that we have had in the past.

When we smell the briny, salty smell of the ocean, it might remind us of traveling with our family. Tasting a pie like the ones Aunt Betty used to make, we may find ourselves really missing her. Smelling and tasting, we may feel "mixed feelings," some sadness that special moments have ended, or maybe happiness that we feel them again. Either way, we're likely to be very aware of feelings we have had before.

Touching

Petting a kitten, holding a child's hand, walking barefoot on a rag rug—all these experiences are memorable because of our sense of touch. When we hold or touch something, the sensation connects directly with our bodies and minds. Memories of what we have touched give reminiscing an intimate feeling. When we hug someone or hold that person's hand, we are feeling close to him or her. We can remember how that felt.

4. "Pump-Priming" Activities to Strengthen Memory

Reminiscing together is fun! When we exercise our ability to remember, sharing past experiences with others becomes more enjoyable. Our memories respond best when we are relaxed, yet alert. Memory fitness adds greater joy and meaning to our lives. What better way to exercise our memory ability than to have fun remembering?

A Note about Limitations

When it comes to remembering, you may discover that you have some limitations. It's not important how much we remember. What is important is that our experiences and our memories of them make us uniquely ourselves. Reminiscing together—sharing experiences with others—has a healing power. As we share experiences, we find connections with friends and our community. We rediscover who we are so that we can pass along the gift of our experiences to our children and grandchildren.

Whatever your reasons are for reading this book, feel free to skip around—to explore the topics that interest you most.

Howard I. Thorsheim, Ph.D.
Bruce B. Roberts, Ph.D.

A Suggestion for Using This Book

1. Look over the Contents page and mark each chapter you would like to read.

2. As you read the chapter you selected, put a check by ideas that "ring a bell" for you based on your own experiences.

3. Get together with others to share what you think, feel, and experience as you read each chapter.

Chapter 1

Reminiscing Together: Sharing Memories of Life Experiences

Throughout history, people have used storytelling to pass on values and to promote kinship in the process of living. Greek legends tell us how heroes nobly survived wars and famine. Bible parables teach us how to treat our neighbors with patience and kindness. Stories of Native Americans and pioneers demonstrate how our ancestors worked and lived in a world without modern luxuries. In our lives this very moment, we are meeting challenges that will astonish tomorrow's youths. These younger ones can learn a lot from our example.

Whether our experiences are of joys or frustrations, each of us has many stories to tell. As we relate our experiences, others learn from us and feel permitted to share theirs. Before long, stories recreating times of our lives begin to flow as a spring flows from its source.

Remember flying a kite on a warm, breezy spring day? Or skipping arm-in-arm with friends through puddles left by May showers?

Reminiscing lets us relive our favorite memories. It may instill in us a sense of inner peace or belonging. Reminiscing may fill us with pride in our heritage. Or it may help us rediscover the expectant joy of our youth. Whatever our emotional response, reminiscing together prompts us to remember.

TRUST-BUILDING

We often find that common experiences link our lives with those of others. Such linking experiences form a foundation for friendship; the more we reminisce together, the more we find ourselves caring about one another. Perhaps we feel good about ourselves, too, as we learn that others are uplifted by our friendship and support.

Strong, lasting friendships are built with trust—the kind of trust that is nurtured by respect for each other's life experiences, thoughts, and feelings. We can learn to trust people whose lives are very different from ours if they respect our experiences.

Knowing how much to share about what has happened in our lives depends on how safe we feel to do so. Each of us has a sense of how trust builds gradually with friendship. So we can depend on our own good judgment about how much we feel comfortable sharing.

REMEMBERED SADNESS, REMEMBERED JOY

When, through storysharing, we allow others to see into our lives, unexpected feelings may surface—feelings that bring laughter as well as tears. Each of us has blocked out memories of painful experiences. But, in doing so, we've also hidden some joyful memories. To rediscover the happy memories that lie beneath sad ones, we must be willing to risk sharing our true feelings with someone we trust. We must also understand that getting through our sadness is likely to be scary—and to take time.

A young student of ours, Jane, shared the following story about getting to know her grandmother:

✦

Grandma and I have always had talks together. When I see friends my age, they aren't as objective as Grandma is. She looks at my situation from years of experience. Our talks have been so important to me that I've often wondered how they were helping Grandma.

After Grandpa died, Grandma tried to share her sadness with our family. No one else wanted to listen. I found that, because I listened, Grandma felt safe sharing her sadness with me. She talked about missing Grandpa. She also talked about her family's poverty during the Great Depression.

It wasn't easy for Grandma to share such painful memories. It took a lot of time. But eventually Grandma's sadness began to lift. And when it did, she recalled many happy memories she had forgotten. She remembered how close she felt to her family during those tough times. She also recalled the delight of paying only ten cents for ice cream!

Because we spent time together, Grandma was able to share her happy memories as well as her sad ones. Now it's much easier for her to remember the many good things that have happened to her.

✦

Jane's story shows the value of sharing life experiences between generations. It was comforting for Jane to learn what her grandmother had gained from her experiences—her wisdom and perspective. And, had it not been for Jane's earnest listening, her grandmother may have kept remembrances of her life's happy moments buried beneath her sadness.

On the other side of sadness, there is joy to be found—and a deeper appreciation for the breadth of our experience. Sharing memories of sadness is much like rowing a canoe through weeds to get to shore. We know the shore is there, though we may not always see it. In a similar way, sad memories may temporarily keep us from recognizing the joys we have known in our lives. We can trust that storysharing will guide us back to our happier memories. When painful memories clear away, our memories of good times will be uppermost in our minds.

TAKING TURNS

By taking turns telling and listening, Jane and her grandmother earned each other's trust. In this way, they shared the activity of reminiscing. Telling and listening are supportive roles that empower each person in the process of storysharing. Our dual roles of telling and listening help us in the following ways:

✦ We feel less alone in our experiences.

✦ We feel respected for our uniqueness.

✦ We learn to trust others.

✦ We gain wisdom about our experiences.

✦ We affirm the progress we're making.

STORY-LISTENING

We listen for many reasons. Sometimes we're moved to understand another person's experience. Other times, we're looking for the common links between our experiences and the storyteller's. Or we may hope to learn something new.

When we know others well, both of us find that we're listening alternately and attentively to each other. At such times, we're especially aware of the bond between us.

Each time we converse with someone, we can practice listening skills. Contrary to what we might think, listening must be an active role. Active listening, predictably, has a positive impact on our talks with others. Let's review some simple and effective listening skills:

- ✦ Repeat short summaries of what your friend has said.

  For example, "I hear you saying that you like it when others learn your name."

- ✦ Ask open questions that encourage your friend to talk more, such as "Would you say more about that?" This way, your friend can't answer simply Yes or No.

- ✦ Reflect on feelings. For example, say things like "That sounded like a happy time."

As you listen, try to picture what your friends looked like at the times they're speaking about. Imagine, too, the setting—where the experience took place. If necessary, ask for more details. For example, if your friend tells of a special day or event, ask who else was there, what happened, what the weather was like, what the surroundings looked like on that day. Prod your friend's imagination. When you use active listening skills, you are helping your friend to remember more.

These tips can serve as memory pegs upon which to recall details of experiences. Such mental pictures help us pay attention as we reminisce. The more we form mental pictures of our friends' experiences, the more active an interest we take in them. All the while, we're strengthening our ability to remember!

INVOLVEMENT IN OUR COMMUNITY

Our research shows that people who are involved in their community gain significant health benefits. They have less stress. They trust others more and are able to take the risk of initiating new friendships.

To benefit from community involvement, we must care about what happens to others. We must know and use skills that will help us link up with them. One of these skills is listening actively to our friends. Another skill is remembering names. Recalling and using our friends' names is important. Each time we call someone by name, we are telling that person that he or she matters to us. The more we become involved with others, the more they will share with us and ask us to be involved with them.

Active involvement with others can actually save lives. A friend of ours shared a story about how a group of people met together each Friday night at a local restaurant. One night a shy man named Bill was missing. One couple decided to go to Bill's house to see if he was there. Indeed, Bill was home, but he was lying unconscious on the floor of his kitchen. The couple called an ambulance to transport Bill to a hospital. He could have died if his friends had not been concerned about him.

Bill's story is a touching example of how friends need one another. If we don't have a group that we meet with regularly, it's a good idea to start one. Such groups of people who share common experiences or concerns are forming rapidly in our country—and with good reason. These groups, called mutual help groups, provide an effective, supportive way to help ourselves and others. (Appendix A provides information about programs developed by ACTION, the federal volunteer agency, which suggests ways elders can volunteer their skills and experience in the community. The ideas suggested by these programs can be adapted for use in many ways.)

Here are some ideas on how to start a group that will meet to reminisce and have fun together. The steps are easy.

1. Broach the idea of sharing life experiences when you are with your friends. (You may turn to the "Pump Primer" activities in Chapter 8 for help.)

2. Ask people to read and discuss chapters of this book *Reminiscing Together* with you.

3. Select a group leader who is not viewed as a memory expert, but rather as someone who just enjoys reminiscing.[1]

4. Set group guidelines about accepting one another, sharing responsibility, and creating safety together.

5. Everybody should have the option of talking or remaining silent.[2]

As we join with others to reminisce together, we are able to strengthen our community memory. You've heard the saying "Two heads are better than one." Each of us remembers some parts of an experience we have had together. But, oh, how rich and flexible our minds can be when we share our reminiscences!

We'd like to end this chapter with a poem from our friend Martha:

To Memory

I have passed four-score years—
a long time, a great deal of living.

I am that child that went forth
and all that I saw, heard, and felt
became part of me.

Thanks to memory
I am aware of much of the living.

I remember happiness as a child—
security, support, love.

I remember brothers and sisters,
two of each.

New relationships.

I remember reaching out into the community—
school: remembering, so important!

Then, teaching—
remembering names, needs, and capacities
of many individuals at once.

Using memory to collect facts.

I remember friends and students—
memory enhanced the relationships.

I remember love—the beauty, the ecstasy!

Then—how it hurt!

Forgetting helped time dissolve the hurt and the
pain of defeated expectation.

I remember reaching out
to faraway communities,
learning to know many people.

I remember them as human beings like myself—
they remember, too.

So much of the past is with me today.

Is there danger that I may use memory
to neglect the present?

Shouldn't memory assist me
to be more helpful, more understanding, today?

Thank you, God,
for the gifts of memory, and forgetting.

Help me to use them wisely!

Martha M. Mattson

1. See our essay Empowering Leadership (1988) for tips on leadership. Available from the authors.

2. These ideas are adapted from the Thorsheim and Roberts book, *Mutual Helping*, 1984.

Chapter 2

How Memory Works

We began this book by describing how a good memory helps us learn, adapt to change, and make friends. We identified memories as thoughts, feelings, and experiences we hold within us. Memory can also mean the ability to store and retain thoughts, feelings, and experiences. Some things we remember for only a short time. Others, we remember much longer.

We will never have a perfect memory. Nor will we remember every thought, feeling, or life experience. All the same, our minds are much more powerful than any computer! We may envy computers for their "ability" to call up details quicker than we can. But computers cannot

25

reminisce. Nor can they describe places they have been or people they have known. Any computer could have stored the words for this page, but it took several unique people to prepare this book.

The older we become, the more experience we gain. We're all able to recall memories of experiences, even though our skill at remembering may have changed.

SHORT-TERM MEMORY

Imagine a funnel with a container beneath it. Our short-term memory is much like a funnel that holds liquid for a few seconds on its way to a container.

Our long-term memory is much like a container that actually bottles, or stores, details and thoughts we would like to remember. Long-term memory stretches beyond the few seconds typical of short-term memory. Through long-term memory we bottle, or store, information in our minds for minutes, hours, days, and years.

Just as a funnel helps get juice into a bottle, our short-term memory helps get things into long-term memory. Short-term memory helps us remember things, as needed, for a few seconds. Short-term memory helps us hang on to details—like phone numbers or new friends' names—long enough to use them or to remember them. If we had only long-term memory, our minds would be filled with useless information!

Short-term memory is also known as working memory or immediate memory. It's the memory we must strengthen to remember new bits of information.

If information doesn't make it to our long-term memory before about thirty seconds, we do not retain, or bottle it, in our long-term memory. If, for example, we try to recall a telephone number, and someone interrupts us before we use the number, we will no doubt forget it. It's as though information in our short-term memory funnel evaporates before we can bottle it.

How Can We Improve Our Short-term Memory?

To improve short-term memory, we must pay careful attention to how things get into this "memory funnel."

Paying attention means to observe and to focus on what we would like to recall.

For example, often we put things into short-term memory the way we toss things into a "junk drawer." In junk drawers, we throw in odds and ends without any organization. Imagine such a drawer. It might have scissors, or some string tied in a ball. Perhaps there's a shoelace—not two, but one. And maybe an eraser so dry and hard it tears paper instead of erasing!

If we tried to find a paper clip in such a drawer, we might become a bit overwhelmed. Though we may know it's there, we can't find it easily, so it's as good as lost.

Fortunately, we can learn to store special information in a more organized way. Here are some helpful new ways to pay attention to what we notice, so that later, we can easily draw it out of our memory!

As you notice something:

Connect it with something else it reminds you of.

Picture it as it "funnels" through your mind.

Repeat its name several times as you are putting it into your short-term memory.

Memory Overload or "Overfilling the Funnel"

We can pour liquid only so fast through a funnel. If we go too fast, our efforts are wasted. What we pour will run over the top and down the sides! Our short-term memory "funnel" works much the same way. Our short-term memory "funnel" may be large or small. But whatever its size, it can only hold about five to nine chunks of information—about the number of digits in a telephone number—at any given time.

Short-term memory overload occurs when we try to put too much in our short-term memory all at once.

Let's try something together. Close your eyes and remember the number "3." Can you remember it without any trouble? Probably so, because it's well below the limit of five to nine chunks of information.

Now remember 3 digits: 4, 8, and 9. That's not so hard, is it?

Now we'll go to 5 digits: 2, 5, 6, 8, and 9.

If you can repeat those, you're doing better than many eighteen-year-olds!

Now memorize these six digits: 3, 4, 0, 6, 1, and 7. Close your eyes and say them back. We're feeling our funnels start to run over. Are you? If we go to nine digits, the overload may make anyone's short-term memory funnel run over!

MEMORY RECALL AND RECOGNITION

We've all heard the expression, "It's on the tip of my tongue, but I can't remember!" That tip of the tongue experience happens to all of us. Sometimes when we stop trying to remember something, it will come to us. Our friend Clarence called this experience "pop-up memories." Clarence said:

> It's probably always been around, I suppose, but I notice it more now. You know, I just can't think of something, and then, all of a sudden it will pop up!

✦

Pop-up memories may come seconds or days later—even when we're not trying to think of them. In fact, sometimes the best way to remember something is to stop trying so hard.

Both recall and recognition memory help us bring back information we need when we need it.

Recall memory is the result of searching for what you know.

For instance, try to recall details in an old photograph you once had of you as a child. The details you remember and see in your mind's eye are examples of recall memory. With recall memory, we're not relying on clues to help us remember—we're relying on our memory alone. This makes recall memory quite a challenge.

Recognition memory is identifying something as familiar. Perhaps it's something that we have seen or heard before.

It's easiest to recognize a detail if we've seen it before. We have often looked at a certain baby photograph and recognized clearly a favorite blossoming apple tree in the background. Yet, if asked to describe the details of that yard without the picture handy, we may find it harder to recall the apple tree.

The more clues we have—like those provided by the photograph—the easier it is to recognize familiar things—the yard with the blossoming apple tree, for example. When we have certain clues, we think of other, related clues that help even more. Recognition memory is much easier than recall memory, remembering something "out of the blue."

Being able to recognize something as familiar means that your recognition memory is working well, even when you rely upon clues and prompts.

To practice recognition memory, look at an object in your surroundings. For example, ask yourself, "Is that a picture I've seen before, or not?" If you get a feeling of familiarity, that means you are using recognition memory.

If we have visual pictures of our experiences—like photographs—it is easier to remember the experience. It is also true that if we are trying to remember a particular experience, it helps to imagine in our mind's eye what it looks like.

WAYS TO REMEMBER BETTER

A friend of ours, Catherine Sears, gave us permission to relate this experience she had.

✦

While I was visiting relatives in California last week, I was told that on the next day we were going to be with some friends whom I'd known during the war years. They were from my former home, Madison, Wisconsin.

Since I couldn't sleep very well that night, I began thinking of the old neighborhood, the houses in the block. Then I began thinking of the names of the people in each of those houses. In the quiet of the night, each house and each person living in that house seemed to come vividly to me.

"My," I thought, "what fun we'll have tomorrow."

Just going through that mental exercise, with logical, undisturbed, but disciplined thinking, made me realize the value of repetition.

Disciplined, logical thinking seems to come best when you're relaxed. And, it was fun besides!

✦

We all have many tasks to do. How often do you have several things you need and want to remember? Perhaps you want to call your friend Sally, pick up flowers, iron your shirt, and arrive at Sally's at 8:00 P.M. Yet you don't want to overload your memory!

Here are some ways to remember better.

Taking a Memory Walk

Thousands of years ago, Greek and Roman orators associated locations with things they wanted to remember. They called this strategy "The Method of Locations."

Francis Galton, an English scientist, revived this strategy as he was studying intelligence in the last century. Galton called it "taking a memory walk" because, as he memorized lists, he would imagine himself taking his favorite walk. He thought about a path or walk that was familiar to him—familiar enough so that he could shut his eyes and see his pathway.

Here's how Galton learned things "by heart." It can work for you, too! Now recall our activity list. Imagine that Galton was trying to remember four activities.

1. Call Sally.
2. Get some flowers.
3. Iron shirt.
4. Be there at 8:00.

In his mind, Galton would imagine walking to the door of his room and also think about the first thing he wanted to recall, call Sally. In his mind's eye, he'd put a telephone on that door and imagine himself calling, "Helloooo, Sally!" To remember to buy flowers, he would imagine flowers outside the door in the hallway. To remember to iron his shirt he would picture the flowers on an ironing board. The fourth thing to remember is the time 8:00. He would imagine himself seeing a big "8" on each stair he walked down. Later, when Galton wanted to remember his tasks, he would envision himself going to his door, calling Sally on the imaginary phone, finding flowers by the door—on the ironing board, and finding "8's" on the stairs. He would then remember to call Sally, buy flowers, iron his shirt, and meet Sally at 8:00.

By using the memory walk, we can remember all kinds of lists. We can remember groceries, dates, even names. All we need to do is imagine a location for each item on our list. The more items we want to remember, the longer the walk—until there's a place for everything on our list. To remember different sets of things—and keep from getting them mixed up with other sets of things—just use a different "walk."

Peg Words

Favorite sayings, or "jingles," can act as pegs on which to "hang" items to remember.

Here's an example of a popular jingle used to remember lists.

> *One is a bun*
> *Two is a shoe*
> *Three is a tree*
> *Four is a door*
> *Five is a hive*
> *Six are sticks*
> *Seven is heaven*
> *Eight is a gate*
> *Nine is wine*
> *Ten is a hen.*

Now repeat the jingle to yourself, filling in the missing words:

> *One is a _____,*
> *Two is a _____,*
> *Three is a _____,*
> *Four is a _____,*
> *etc.*

The missing words—bun, shoe, tree, door—act as "mental pegs" on which to hang items to remember, such as to call Sally, buy flowers, iron a shirt, and be at Sally's at 8:00.

Remember to hang your memory item on one peg at a time!

1. *One is a bun. Call Sally.*
We must think of a mental picture that combines a bun with telephoning. Incidentally, research has shown that the more unusual your mental picture, the better it will be remembered. Imagine, for instance, a telephone shaped like a hamburger bun. What a comical image! How could we possibly forget it? Let's go a step further.

2. *Two is a shoe. Buy flowers.*
Imagine a shoe filled with flowers.

3. *Three is a tree. Iron shirt.*
Picture a tree branch with an ironed shirt hanging from a branch on a clothes hanger.

4. *Four is a door. Meet Sally at 8:00.*
Picture a clock with its hands on 8:00 carved on Sally's door.

The more unusual and humorous your images are, the more likely you are to remember them!

Mnemonic Devices

Mnemonic (pronounced "knee-MA-nick" without the beginning "m" sound) is any kind of helper for remembering a piece of information. Stories can be mnemonics. So can pictures, sounds, aromas, and the feeling of touch. How do we remember such an odd word as "mnemonic"? Because the word begins with the sound "knee," we can imagine a mother's knee with a child perched on it. The second syllable is pronounced "MA" as in "Ma and Pa Kettle." The last syllable is pronounced like the boy's name, Nick. Can you think of other ways to remember, using mnemonics?

Imagery

Imagery is the art of making mental pictures. We have talked about using visual images, such as printed words of a song, bun-shaped telephones, and landmarks on our favorite walks. Sounds, smells, tastes, and our sense of touch bring images and memories to mind as well. That's why we have devoted the next four chapters to ways that we can remember by using our senses.

Chapter 3

Seeing and Remembering

Our senses—seeing, hearing, taste, smell, and touch—are the building blocks of memory. Of these building blocks, our sense of vision helps us take in the largest amount of information. Our ability to see colors, shapes, textures, movements, and light makes our experiences—and our memories of them—vibrant and rich.

We store what we see in our mind's eye, or imagination. If you close your eyes for a second, you can still see the words "mind's eye" that you've just read. Our eyes are a superior camera, capturing images of our life experiences. This very moment, you are taking a snapshot of what you see.

As we recall experiences, we often see—or "picture" in our minds—details that have left a strong impression on us. It's as though we are looking at a photograph. We might actually have a favorite photograph that helps us keep such details firmly in mind.

Our memories of life experiences are like a series of pictures on a wall. Each picture records an instant of time. Each is joined together with the other pictures that "capture" an experience.

CLARA'S STORY

A friend of ours, Clara Paulsen, gave us permission to share a unique experience she had:

✦

Up near the Turtle Mountains, not far from the Canadian border in north central North

Dakota, was our farm where I grew up—just twelve miles from Bottineau. There my parents, siblings, and I enjoyed many a happy time! We loved our house with its gingerbread trimmings, and big screened-in porches, and a big yard where we played croquet, softball, and penny sticks (also called "whipple"). And we'd swing high in our strong swings—my father would push us.

One day when I was twelve years old and my brother Cliff was fourteen, he and I were home alone. The rest of the family was away. Soon (as was often the case in those days), a horse and buggy pulled up. Out stepped a man carrying the most interesting equipment that you can imagine. He was a traveling photographer. He wanted to take a picture of our house there on the farm.

He said, "I'll give you, as a premium, a large, beautiful framed picture of the U.S. Capitol in Washington, D.C."

So, we innocently signed some papers, and he took the picture. Off he drove.

Weeks later we received the promised picture together with a lovely, colored picture of our house in a large, oval frame. But, included was a bill for $27.00!

Fortunately, our parents never chided us for our childhood blunder. Now I have the picture on the wall in my apartment. It is a source of endless pleasure, as I remember from time to time many an incident from my more youthful days.

✦

Stimulating Memories with Photographs

Each of us has a photograph that reminds us of a special time we have enjoyed. Perhaps it's one of a memorable Thanksgiving years ago. Perhaps that was the Thanksgiving we saw a favorite aunt for the first time in years. Maybe it was our job to check the nicely browning turkey in the oven. Or maybe we think of sitting in a big, overstuffed chair after dinner—overstuffed too! We might think most about the moment we sat at the table to eat. Perhaps we can picture where everyone was sitting—dad, mother, sisters, brothers, aunts, uncles, and a grandparent or two. If we start with that mental picture, then other events of such a day may come to mind as well. We might even recall some of the feelings or thoughts we had at the time.

Photographs can often remind us of experiences in our lives like nothing else can. Find a favorite photograph and think of experiences it brings to mind. Photographs are likely to include a variety of reminders from your past. They might be of events, scenes, people, or specific objects. It is helpful if you notice the details in the picture, like the expression on people's faces, where the event was happening, and what time of day or year it might have been. If you are in the picture, or somewhere nearby, can you remember where you were sitting or standing, what someone was saying, or how you felt?

Here are some examples of the kinds of pictures that may remind you of events and experiences in your life. Take a look. Perhaps they will suggest other pictures that will help you connect with some of your own experiences.

Rural or city landscapes	*A tractor*
Family gatherings	*A dog with puppies*
Baseball games	*A blizzard*
Dolls	*A beach scene*
Department stores	*An iron frame bed*
A freight yard	*A steam engine locomotive*
A movie theater crowd	*A picture of Franklin Roosevelt*
A country church	*Your first washing machine*

Whatever photographs you have around can stimulate memories.

When looking at the pictures, let your thoughts meander like a brook. It may take time for you to remember parts of experiences. That's to be expected.

In Chapter 4, we talk about how helpful it is to share experiences with others. Sharing

photographs with friends is fun and a supportive
activity. Invite friends over—and ask them
to bring along some of their favorite
photographs—so that you may share pictures
with one another. Pick a time that is likely to be
free from interruptions. With friends, you can
"think out loud" about photographs as you look at
them. Make sure to have proper lighting so that
you can see well. The more comfortable you are,
the more likely you will be able to recall
experiences. Round up a pencil or two to make
notes about your pictures on the back of them if
you wish to.

As we look at photographs, it is almost as
though our eyes are behind the lens of the camera
that first took the picture. When we see pictures
of moments we have enjoyed, we travel back in
time. There's no limit to the experiences our eyes
can help us remember.

Chapter 4

Hearing and Remembering

Our ears introduce us to a whole new way to recall our experiences. We can hear memories as well as see them. In Chapter 3 we talked about how a favorite song brings thoughts to mind. Thoughts of a favorite song might recreate the sound of that song in our minds. Perhaps remembering a song stirs memories of other sounds, like voices of friends.

When we listen to a song, and hear it as a song rather than disconnected notes, our memory ability is working. The notes that are played are retained in our "short-term memory funnel" just long enough for us to keep them in our "mind's ear."

Often, as we listen to a song and pay attention to what we are hearing, the rest of the song will come to us. You might recall the first line of the song "Down by the Old Mill Stream."

If you recalled the phrase "where I first met you," you remembered!

SONGS AND MEMORY

With help from friends, we can remember titles of our favorite songs. A lot of memories—some happy, some sad—may come to mind as we recall Bing Crosby singing "Brother, Can You Spare a Dime?" from the 1930s and the days of the Great Depression. Perhaps we'll hear in our minds the voices of our family and friends imitating Bing Crosby. Our "hearing memory" might be so vivid that we can almost hear the crooner's actual voice.

You and your friends may come up with titles of other favorite songs. Here are some "pump primers" to get you started:

"The Good Ship Lollipop"　　*"Good Night, Irene"*

"Sentimental Journey"　　*"Don't Fence Me In"*

"Washington Post March"　　*"Blue Moon"*

"Stars and Stripes Forever"　　*"Alexander's Ragtime Band"*

"Don't Sit Under the Apple Tree"　　*"It's Been a Long, Long Time"*

These songs may bring to mind people you were with when you heard the songs before. When you hear them, imagine where you were, what you were doing, or the particular time you heard them.

RADIO SHOWS

Hearing favorite songs might remind us of early radio programs we enjoyed. Remember "Fibber McGee and Molly" (and their closet)? Or "Baby Snooks" (with Fanny Brice)? How about Edgar Bergen and Charlie McCarthy? With a friend you may choose to come up with some of your other favorite programs. If you are sharing this book with someone younger than you, talking about favorite radio programs promises great fun! Today's youth can really learn and benefit from time with you. Maybe you can help create a memorable time together by telling about those fine programs of yesteryear!

Perhaps you can reminisce about the following programs:

Jack Benny
Corliss Archer
The Great Gildersleeve
Walter Winchell ("Mr. and Mrs. America")
Lowell Thomas and the News ("So long! Until Tomorrow!")
Edward R. Murrow ("This...is London...!")
The Lux Radio Theater
Your Hit Parade

Do any particular commercial jingles come to mind from those early shows?

USING SOUNDS TO IMAGINE A PLACE

Bringing sounds to mind can "transport" us to favorite places or settings. Hearing the gurgle of water in an aquarium can bring to mind sitting near a waterfall or a brook. Think about the sound of dry leaves rustling. Does it transport you to a breezy, spring morning, or an eerie Halloween night? Listening to ocean sounds, or the sounds of a cleansing rain, helps some people relax. There are now many tapes available with a variety of recorded sounds, which can help us relax and rest our minds. They also can help us remember experiences and people.

Here are some examples of sounds that may bring to mind experiences we've known.

Country Sounds

A rooster's morning crow
Cattle walking across a barn floor
Meadowlarks singing on a telephone line

Cows mooing while waiting to be milked
A howling wind
A steam engine whistling in the distance
Fresh, crunchy snow

City Sounds

Favorite next-door neighbors' voices
Subway trains and streetcars
Happy crowds
Horns and busy streets
Children playing in the park
Spring baseball
A construction crew working on a street

The more we can hear, the more we can put into our short-term memory funnel! And then, of course, the more we can remember in general. Sounds, music, and voices greatly enhance our memories.

Chapter 5

Aromas and Memory

Our experiences are often linked to aromas. Aromas are fragrances or flavors that are usually quite pleasant. They are tied to our ability to smell and to taste. The beauty and richness of our memories is very often tied to aromas. Aromas are likely to help us recall favorite experiences. The smells of fresh-baked bread, a roast in the oven, and fresh coffee make our mouths water. They also remind us of sharing meals with friends and family.

AROMA MEMORY TAGS

Aromas can help us remember experiences and people. Many pleasant times we have spent with friends have aroma memory tags associated with them. Examples include the fragrance of special perfumes or clean linen. One person said to us, "I can still remember the fresh smell of clean bed sheets and towels in the wicker clothes basket my mother brought in after hanging them out to dry on the backyard clothesline."

Remembering an experience can also bring a certain aroma to mind. Memories of Christmas may make us recall the smells of popcorn, gingerbread, vanilla extract, or burning wood in the fireplace. Stop for a moment to think of a special holiday. What aromas come back to you?

Anything that has an aroma is giving off molecules, or parts of itself. When we smell an aroma, we are actually smelling the tiny molecules. That is why our senses of taste and smell are often called *chemical senses*. Our ability to smell and to taste is so sensitive that it only takes a few molecules of an aroma to "perk" our memory. It is common for memories to come to us quickly when we smell an aroma.

Aromas are closely tied to our sense of taste. Remember having a cold and not being able to taste very well? There's a strong link between aromas and appetite.

Exchanging favorite recipes with friends is a unique way to pass on our experiences of aromas. When passing along a recipe we may wish to tell about when we first used it. There are many interesting stories about recipes. When you smell spaghetti sauce cooking, it might remind you of the abundance of tomatoes in a summer garden. Perhaps Grandmother's turkey dressing tasted so good because she let it brown a little in the pan.

CHOOSE AN AROMA

The following list suggests aromas that are sure to stimulate your memory. What are some of your

favorite aromas? Ask a friend about hers or his.
What aromas are you enjoying at this very moment?

Alfalfa	*Onion*
Fried Chicken	*Peanut butter*
Cedar	*Dill pickle*
Cinnamon	*Popcorn*
Fresh air	*Smoke*
Lilac	*Mothballs*
Lumber	*Salty air*
A new car's upholstery	*Diesel fuel*
Turpentine	*Pine trees*

Mixing Senses

At times senses become mixed with one another.
Some people may hear a sound but think of a
certain color. They might imagine "light yellow"
when they hear a high-pitched sound, or "brown"
when a sound is low-pitched. Others might taste
something and describe it with a term used for
sound. For example, they might describe gravy as
having a "rich, deep" flavor. This ability to
experience something in one sense and describe
it in another is called synesthesia. Synesthesia
does not happen often, but when it does, it's sure
to provide us with "memory tags."

Scientists are only beginning to understand
just how much aromas help to strengthen
memory. What is known is that they add a rich
dimension to our lives.

Chapter 6

Touch and Memory

So many of our memories are tied to experiences of touch.

John Sorenson told us this experience about when he was a youngster.

I would take an ear of field corn and try to get the kernels of corn out. It was always hard to get out the first kernel, but after that it became easier. I would wiggle a kernel back and forth in the extra space I could find and pretty soon it would come out—just like a tooth. Then the kernel next to it could be wiggled easier since there was the extra space from the kernel already out—it would go more easily.

After the first row had been removed, I
would take a bit of a different grip on the
ear—which up until then I had been working
with my fingers. I would use the thick part of
my thumb—next to my palm—and kind of
"roll" the row next to the empty space into
the vacancy left by the first row.

Have you ever done that?

Another friend told us about an experience
living in the city.

✦

We would play hopscotch on the cement
sidewalk. We would find a piece of chalk
if we could, but more often than not, we
would find a stone that we called a "writing
stone," probably sandstone, and rub that
on the sidewalk, making the lines. The sense
of touch I remember is having to press the
writing stone so hard in order to make a
mark. I remember the vibrating it did
and how that felt as I rubbed it across
the sidewalk.

✦

For Dorothy Goth, it is the human touch she most remembers.

Silent sharing is important to me. Sympathy expressed with a handclasp is comforting. Praise shown by a pat on the back may be more meaningful than effusive verbal praise. Affection shown by a hug is for real. Feelings shown silently may be remembered for a long time.

As Dorothy points out, it's hard to forget the loving touch of someone dear to us. We might even associate things we smell, taste, see, or hear with precious moments of hugging someone we care about. Whether we are hugging a friend, child, or grandchild, we are sure to savor the way that person looked, what was said, or any fragrance she or he was wearing. Perhaps when we see photographs of these people again, we will remember their smile or the joy we felt hugging them.

Our entire skin surface contains special organs called touch "receptors." Some of these receptors respond to pressure, others to heat, and others to cold. They are particularly sensitive to changes. Many of our memories are tied to temperatures we feel or to things we touch. When the weather suddenly turns warm after days of a cold winter, our thoughts may turn, too—to memories of summer vacations with our family. If we wiggle our toes inside our shoes, we may recall walking barefoot through grass or ocean sand.

THE MEMORY OF TOUCH

The special memory for touch is called haptic memory. Haptic memory includes memory for shapes, textures, and forms.

We invite you to use your memory of touch to bring to mind these favorite things you might have felt:

Smooth, varnished wood   *Starched cloth*

Rough stucco   *Sand*

A furry kitten   *Touches of love*

Together with friends, use your imagination to think of others. Pay attention to what surfaces feel like. Touch pieces of furniture, the wall, or the light switch. Notice how your sense of touch helps you remember how one texture is different from another.

'LEARNING YOUR ORANGE'

Here's an interesting way to demonstrate the power of *haptic* memory with a group of friends:

1. Form a group of four or five people and sit around a table.

2. Find an orange for each person. On each orange, mark a number with a felt marker and put all oranges on the table.

3. Everyone should put on a blindfold (scarves or handkerchiefs work well). Then each person should take one of the oranges.

4. Next, each person is invited to "learn your orange." Perhaps it has a groove or a dimple. Maybe the shape is round or elongated. Everyone will get a chance to identify his or her orange by its shape and uniqueness.

5. When people have had a few minutes to "learn their orange," the oranges can be collected and put on a table.

6. While still blindfolded, each person then gets a chance to find his or her orange.

People can swap oranges back and forth with neighbors if they wish while they are discovering "their" orange. If this activity is done with no more than five or six people, everyone will be surprised at how well they are able to do. To form smaller groups, large groups can be subdivided. The more oranges there are, the more difficult the memory task becomes.

So far in this book, we have talked about how important it is to share experiences together, what we call *reminiscing together.* Reminiscing together helps us make and retain relationships with others that are meaningful and healthy for us and our friends. Memory is an important tool for remembering the life experiences we want to share.

We have talked about how our senses—seeing, hearing, smelling, tasting, and touching—play an important role in remembering. It is important to be honest with ourselves. We may not always remember specific details we would like to just as Howard forgot about his car (our introductory story). However, it is important to give ourselves credit for how well our memories **are working** in so many ways. Shared life experiences are a valuable resource as persons of all ages are reminiscing together.

Chapter 7

Being Honest about Limitations

Remembering and forgetting are qualities of our being *living humans.* We don't talk about a tree forgetting, although a tree also is a living thing. One night with a group of friends, we heard someone mention that it was a gift to be able to remember. Someone else replied that it also was a gift to be able to forget.

As one friend said:

✦

It's impossible and unnecessary to remember everything. In fact, forgetting some of the pain connected to some memories is a blessing.

✦

With the very best effort and intentions, we cannot always remember as well as we would like to. We may believe we remember more than we do. We may even pretend to remember something we don't. All of us play this game of pretending no matter what our age.

Most of us learned to pretend as little children when adults used words we didn't know. As adults we may smile, or nod, and say, "yes, I remember," when we don't really remember at all.

We may even argue about a fact that we're not sure of.

One friend of ours told us about a man who seemed to be having a hard time keeping facts straight. He was once in charge of a department of many people at a bank and wanted his memory to work as it did then.

Our friend said,

✦

One day when talking about football, he asked me who his favorite pro-football team would play next. When I said "Wisconsin," he started yelling that Wisconsin didn't have a pro team and that I was impossible to talk with. When I tried to tell him that the Wisconsin team was the Green Bay Packers,

he said he thought I meant college teams,
and that I always think I'm right.

✦

Our friend said that he didn't mind the man's outbursts because he was used to them. But he wished the man could accept that we all forget now and then—and not take his resentment at being forgetful out on others.

Distrust of others is sometimes a painful result of forgetting. Yet the choice to distrust someone, rather than to think of solutions together—or to ask for help—only increases our loneliness.

It isn't easy to admit our changing ability to remember. That admission demands that we accept our own limitations—and accept limitations of others too. We can find support if we are willing to be open, honest, and respectful with one another.

Physical limitations can *put a lid* on our short-term memory funnels. As we mentioned in Chapter 2, our short-term memory has a limited capacity. Memory that does not make it through the short-term memory funnel will not be bottled into our long-term memory. But we may not understand that one reason we may seem to have difficulty with memory is that we may have a disability.

WHEN OUR VISION CHANGES

Seven out of eight persons over the age of forty-five find it necessary to wear glasses. Because of this, visual disabilities are easier for our friends to recognize. Friends help us keep track of how well our vision is working. Sometimes they'll be honest enough to tell us whether or not our vision is functioning as it did before.

If your vision is changing, you may find that there are things you don't seem to remember. Perhaps you didn't see them in the first place.

Imagine the following conversation:

"Robert, do you remember when Frank waved at you and you didn't wave back?"

Unless Robert realizes that he didn't even see Frank, Robert might find himself saying,

"I don't remember, no."

Robert's friend would be helpful if he said,

"Robert, perhaps you didn't see Frank. Is that possible?"

Robert's friend is helping Robert recognize that his vision is changing. By asking Robert if he saw Frank, he is helping Robert to "see" his experiences better.

Because our eyes are so important in order to remember, we must get help if our vision is changing. Adaptive aids are available to help us lead normal, productive lives when our vision changes.

There are many state and national agencies available to help people who are visually impaired. You may order a catalog from the National Foundation for the Blind that lists many such resources.

American Foundation for the Blind
15 West 16th Street
New York, New York 10011

Talking Books

Materials called "talking books" are available from regional branches of the National Library Service. With a talking book, you can "read the paper" without looking at a single word. Or "read" as you're walking across the living room. There are two ways to hear talking books: through "talking book record players" that can be obtained at no cost from a regional office of the National Library Service in your area; or, in some areas— Minnesota, for example—through radio stations called "Radio Talking Books."

The talking book record player allows you to hear books of all kinds on special records that revolve so slowly that a whole book is contained on six records. A cassette machine is also available to play books and magazines from tapes.

Or you can avail yourself of "Radio Talking Books," reading services accessed from a radio loaned from agencies that serve people who are visually impaired. These radios are different from others in that they use a special portion of an FM radio station that's not being used by any station itself. The talking book radio is pre-set to a single station; you can't dial it to different stations. With the talking book radio, you can listen to the morning newspapers, magazines, news accounts, and books of all kinds. To obtain a talking book radio, check your own state's services for persons with visual impairment.

Appendix B includes other resources for people who are visually impaired.

NOISE

Each one of us hears differently. How good our hearing is depends upon many factors: how relaxed we feel, where we are, how familiar the sounds are to us, and how well our ears are functioning. We *all* have hearing limitations because no one can hear everything all the time. For example, no one can hear well in a factory with pounding machines.

Background noise, like ventilation fans, rustling papers, or a room filled with talking people *masks* other sounds we might like to hear. Noise that masks sounds because it contains all possible sound frequencies is called white noise. An example of white noise might be the whir of an air conditioner.

Our friend Les commented that background music makes it difficult to hear what broadcasters are saying. "Why don't they speak up louder?" asked Les. "With noisy background music, you can't hear a thing people are saying."

Most people have problems hearing if there is background noise. In such cases, we need to be assertive. We can tell broadcasters, for example, that it's difficult to hear announcements when they play background music at the same time.

When noise distracts us, there are ways to help our sense of hearing. First, we can move away from the noise. If we want to hear well, we can move farther away from a fan, machine, or loud music.

Often, we can't escape the noise. But *we can find ways to reduce it.* Fabrics, for example, *absorb* noise rather than reflecting it. Positioning ourselves by a curtain improves our chances of hearing. So does sitting on a couch or near a wall covered with an absorbent cloth.

Trying to hear while seated in the middle of a room, or in a corner with shiny walls, is likely to be frustrating. Sounds may bounce back to us from nearby walls. If you have ever been in a grade school auditorium filled with chattering six-year-olds, you know what we mean. Thank goodness for the curtain on stage! Perhaps the next time you're in such a place, you can situate yourself near fabric that absorbs background noise.

WHEN OUR HEARING CHANGES

According to the National Center for Health Statistics, hearing loss affects over 50 percent of all men over age 65, and 30 percent of all women. Eleanore Devine is a writer, mother, wife, and member of the North Shore Senior Center in Winnetka, Illinois. In the March/April 1987 edition of *SHHH* magazine, she had this to say about hearing loss:

✦

> Losing hearing means losing the beauty of voices and music; the prattle of small children, the small tones of love, but worst of all, it means not knowing what is going on, feeling left out.

✦

Changes in hearing sensitivity take place gradually. Because the process is so gradual, the person experiencing a change in hearing may not be aware that it's happening.

If we have hearing loss, voices sound muffled to us. People may think we forget names or dates when, in fact, we have not heard them.

Loraine DiPietro, director of the National Information Center on Deafness, is hearing impaired. Here is what she told us:

> When I meet new people I sometimes have trouble hearing the names and may use such strategies as asking others to spell their names. The end result is that when I meet these people in the future, I clearly remember them, their faces, the setting, and even our conversation. But, I don't remember names.

✦

If we have a visual impairment, people notice that we're wearing glasses. But people may not see that we're wearing a hearing aid. (If a hearing aid helps us, we can be happy about that. Wearing a hearing aid is no different from wearing glasses to correct our vision.)

If we believe we have a hearing impairment, it's important to let our friends know. Once they know, they can speak more directly to us. Perhaps they can speak louder, too. Often, we need to tell them how to help us. We might ask them to attract our attention by using our names, so we know they'll be saying something important directed toward us. There's no benefit at all to pretending we can hear when we can't.

Appendix C includes communication tips for persons who are hearing impaired. It also lists resources available for individuals who need support in order to hear better.

Chapter 8

Pump Priming to Strengthen Memory

Frank explained:

✦

We had one pump for drinking out in the yard, and a cistern pump on the sink in the kitchen. The outside pump was bigger, with a long curved handle. The pump inside was smaller and had been painted so many times that its surface looked like a smooth enamel. The pump inside was connected to the cistern we used to collect rain water—soft water.

Whenever either pump had not been used for a while, it wouldn't pump, and we always had to pour a couple of cups of water

down the top to "prime the pump." After
that it would pump just fine.

✦

Remembering experiences, thoughts, and
feelings is something like pumping from a cistern.
Priming helps to get the water going. In a similar
way, certain activities help "prime the pump" for
remembering life experiences.

This chapter offers several "pump-priming"
activities to do with others, or alone if you prefer.
The ideas were contributed by people like you
who are interested in sharing life experiences.
These activities are designed to help you use your
memory. You may adapt them as you see fit. The
more relaxed you are and the more fun you have,
the more active your memory is likely to be.

USING PUMP PRIMERS TO HELP REMEMBER NAMES AND INFORMATION

Pump Primer 1: Name Tags and Other Ways to Remember Names

Our friends say that remembering names is one of the most important memory skills they are interested in.

In fact, remembering other people's names is one of the healthiest things you can do for yourself—and for the persons you call by name when you speak with them. No wonder that remembering names is one of the first things people mention when we talk with them about remembering. For example, Harold said:

✦

> I've found it frustrating when I try to recall the name of a place or person, the date, and other details of an event that happened, which at the time I thought was very important.

✦

Sarah, reflecting on the importance of names, commented:

✦

> I find I am so embarrassed when I "go blank"
> in the middle of a conversation—or in
> meeting an acquaintance—and cannot
> remember the name.

✦

This pump primer idea is useful for learning and remembering names:

1. Buy name tags for the people who are getting together (for example, at a family reunion).

2. Use felt markers to print names *VERY LARGE*— large enough that the name can be read twenty feet away.

3. In smaller print, underneath your name, print the origin of your name (if you know it). Names might get their meaning from parents, relatives, places, famous persons, or many other sources.

Gladys Thorsheim suggested writing the name of the town you were born in on the name tag. This is especially helpful in groups where people may not know each other's town of origin.

Gladys said:

> This activity always brings back memories
> and much conversation. In fact, you might
> encourage conversation in other ways, too,
> such as placing names of hometown schools,
> churches, and methods of transportation on
> the name tags.

✦

Here are some other ideas to help others
remember your name:

1. Divide the group into pairs. Each person
   can tell the other something about his or
   her last name. Examples: its meaning,
   ethnic or national origin, changes in
   spelling over the years, how people have
   pronounced it, and so on.

2. You already may have come up with a way
   that helps others recall your name. For
   example, does your name rhyme with
   another word? Share that with your
   friends.

3. Share what is unique about
   you—something that you like to do that is
   fun and perhaps unusual that people could
   associate with your name and you.

Pump Primer 2: Group Photos

1. Get a camera that develops pictures instantly.

2. Take photos of small groups of about a half dozen or so people.

3. Write numbers under each person in the photo who is participating in this activity.

4. On a sheet of paper, number a line for every person who is participating.

5. Have each person write his or her name by the same number as on the picture.

6. The numbers help to match pictures with names. Post the pictures and the sheet of paper on the wall for everyone to see.

Pump Primer 3: Floor Plans

1. Draw the floor plan of a house you lived in as a child.

2. Explain your sketch to a friend: Identify each room. Where did you sleep? Where did you have good times? With whom? Who were some of the people you can remember visiting your house?

Pump Primer 4: Words

1. Sit in a circle. On slips of paper, write words. Any words will do. Put the words into a box. Shake the box and let each person pick a slip of paper without seeing what's on it. Then go around the circle and have each person tell the first thing that comes to mind about his or her word. There is no wrong way to do this! Here are some words that you might use: book, cotton, lake, flower, king, mountain, railroad, storm, river, stove. Add any words you like.

Pump Primer 5: Pictures

Any number of people, divided into small groups of two or three, can enjoy this activity together.

1. Choose a picture or display from your room or from your photo album.

2. Ask a friend to do the same.

3. Bring it along when you next get together with your friend.

4. Each share a story about your own picture.

Pump Primer 6: Shared Courage

1. Each person may think of a time when he or she took a stand on an issue that was important to them.

2. Each person in turn tells his or her story to the others. Omar Otterness said:

First, people think of a time when they took a stand on an issue that was important to them. That is, they search their memories for a situation in which they did something to "stand up" for an important value of theirs.

Then, of course, each person in turn tells her or his story to the others.

Sometimes the stories told are those of courageous action. People's emotions and personal values are brought to the surface. This is usually an effective means of sharing important values, stories of daring and risk, with another in an interesting and exciting manner.

✦

Pump Primer 7: Knitting Together Experiences

This pump primer helps connect a name to an experience told to us by that person:

1. Invite people to sit in a circle.

2. Pass out a few short pieces (about 6 inches long) of colored yarn to each person.

3. Each person thinks of one experience he or she likes to think about.

4. Going around the circle, each person says his or her name and then shares the experience.

5. Anyone in the group who relates to the speaker's experience in any way gives him or her a piece of yarn.

6. Continue around the entire circle.

Pump Primer 8: Newsletter

Several organizations and communities have found that a newsletter is an excellent and fun way to encourage sharing of experiences. The newsletter can include:

1. Short stories from life experiences.

2. A brief sketch about the life of each person who helps put together the newsletter.

3. Favorite ways to use spare time.

4. Dates and times of upcoming events— lectures, concerts, and elderhostel classes— especially those during daylight hours.

5. Tips on health subjects, such as recipes for simple, nutritious foods.

6. Trivia quizzes, especially about the people involved. Examples: Who has a brother in Sioux Falls? Who has four sons?

7. Helpful resources. Examples: tax preparers or special interest clubs.

8. Jokes (not too corny).

9. Humorous cartoons.

10. Pending legislation of importance and interest.

11. Birthplaces of community members.

12. A short item about some bit of remembered history.

13. Names, addresses, and phone numbers of people who are willing to be resources for various kinds of interests.

14. The title of a favorite "oldie but goodie" song—a new one each week.

Remember to pay attention to individuals, not just to the group. NAME NAMES! Keep the newsletter brief.

Pump Primer 9: Storytelling

This activity, is designed to help with recalling names.

1. Find a comfortable room with chairs for your meeting.

2. Get together a group of people who want to know each other's names.

3. On a piece of paper, jot down an experience from your youth. Examples: favorite pets, funny situations, worst chores, or your first school.

4. Tell your first names and experience to the person sitting next to you.

5. Your new friend will then jot down your name and a thing or two about your experience. That way he or she will be able to think of your name and your experience the next time he or she sees you.

6. Your friend will then introduce you by name to the group, telling something about

your experience. (Your friend can look at the jotted notes as a pump primer if he or she wants to. That's OK.)

Here is an example:

I'd like to introduce you to Karen. She told of an experience from a time when she was about three or four. She and her younger brother shared a room in a house in Wisconsin. At night they would get up on the headboards of their beds and look out across the street where a train track crossed right in front of a park across the street. They would enjoy just sitting on the headboards, watching the trains go by.

✦

After each person has introduced his or her neighbor by name and mentioned the experience, you may want to discuss what was gained by doing this pump primer exercise.

Pump Primer 10: Remembering Intentions

1. On a sheet of paper, each person anonymously lists things that he or she intends to do each day on a regular basis but—as we all do— forgets. (Remember, do not write names on the papers.)

2. Collect lists.

3. Everyone moves into groups of three.

4. Lists are randomly distributed, one per person.

5. Each person in turn reads one thing from the list he or she has been given to the two other people.

6. The three group members share— and jot down for later use—tips for recalling intentions.

7. After about ten minutes, each small group can share its ideas with the larger group.

8. If there is interest in doing so, a list of the intentions and tips can be collected, typed, and distributed to all participants as a guide for remembering intentions.

Pump Primer 11: Line Drawing

Bettye Olson of Augsburg College in Minneapolis has developed a good idea using drawings and stick figures. Her "Look...do you see what I see?" is a positive and creative memory-building approach that has been used very successfully with many groups. Here's how it goes:

1. Sketch people who have been important to you.

2. Name and describe them.

3. Tell a story about your sketch.

Any media, pens, pencils, or pastels, can be used. Sketches can be made with very simple line drawings and stick figures. Be imaginative!

Pump Primer 12: Bring a Thing

In a group, each person is asked to bring along a "thing" that reminds him or her of a favorite experience that he or she would be willing to tell about. Example: a favorite stone. Describe where it came from, why it was picked up, who you were with, and what you were doing when you picked it up. It could be any kind of object, but encourage each other to keep the description simple. The goal is not to have the "best thing," but to encourage each other to think about and share memories of experiences that are "primed" by the object you bring. The more others can make a connection with your experience, the more likely they'll be to recall an experience of their own.

PRIMING YOUR OWN PUMP

The following priming activities are designed to help you strengthen your memory on your own.

Pump Primer 13: Recalling Your Own Experiences

1. A diary, even one written years after the events, can help fill in the experiences of a lifetime. Or, look at your souvenirs or mementos (literally "bits of memory"). Ask yourself questions about them and record your answers: "Where did I get that?" "When was it?" "Why did I get it?" "Who was I with?" Sometimes a memento will prime the pump to remember an experience.

2. Look over letters—even receipts and bills— to stimulate memories of experiences related to individuals you care about.

3. Write a list of topics—or ask a family member to write you a list—that you might like to explore in your memory.

June said:

◆

My daughter gave me a list of headings or topics, and asked me to write down anything that came to mind under each one. It really helped to have a list of things that I knew she was interested in knowing about. I found that I wrote down other things as well that were brought to mind by those things she was interested in.

✦

4. At a cardshop or bookstore, find a "Grandmother's" or "Grandfather's" book to record your experiences for grandchildren. They are very popular. You'll find questions to answer. As you write down your answers, your experiences become a gift for a grandchild. These books are terrific pump primers.

Pump Primer 14: The Memory Workbook

1. In a looseleaf notebook, record "vignettes," or scenes, from life around you. Keep them short. With a looseleaf, you can move pages and insert new ones as you please. Periodically, reread what you've written; it will serve as a pump primer for remembering experiences.

2. Write about someone else's present experience. Link it with your own, write down your feelings at the time, and tell details you recall.

Here's an anonymous note someone sent after trying this activity:

✦

I have been thinking about this problem for about a year or so and I think each person has an *inhibition* about putting things *down*—putting it off because it's not properly organized, etc. I have decided to take a looseleaf notebook—and consider it a *workbook*, not in final form—and write only on one side of the page, leaving room thereby to make additions and corrections on the back of the page by references to the front—like footnotes.

Also, I think these vignettes should be short—covering a particular situation without regard to where it fits into the whole scheme of things.

Here is a chance to retell stories we heard from our parents or grandparents— put in everything you can think of—where you were when Grandma told the story, etc. Anything at all that comes to mind should be jotted down. Then there is always room on the back of the page to insert changes or additions. Revisions, tabulating, and organizing can be done later. Even if these changes are never done, at least you have the basic material, and it could be arranged by someone else.

If a person has a tape recorder or dictating machine of any kind, this could be used as a first step—just sit down and dictate the story. I can talk better and faster than I can write. I like to make a few notes and then dictate from this sketchy outline. Once dictated, it can be typed up or left on the tape.

Remembering only a few lines may still be valuable. Don't think any idea is too short to be worth recording.

✦

Pump Primer 15: Remembering Your Family

On the backs of photos of family members and relatives, take time to write down any identifying information you can—for example, anything that describes who it is, when and where the photo was taken, and what was going on. One of our friends said of this pump primer:

✦

Thank you for including this golden bit of advice! We should all do it, beginning with the next picture we take or are given!

✦

Pump Primer 16: Making Gifts of Your Remembering

1. During a holiday celebration, like Christmas, think back to other holidays that you have celebrated and remember. Tell about a special aspect of that special Christmas (or Fourth of July, Hanukkah, birthday).

2. Invite others to do the same.

3. Put together a tape recording, or story, of the experience.

4. Give the tape as a special gift—for a birthday, Christmas, or Hanukkah.

You can also list names of relatives and make a list of who is related to whom. You may wish to list friends whose names have come up in family conversation over the years. Write this list out in your own hand. Make a photocopy for family members. If you do a genealogy, you may wish to include the sources of your information to assist others who may want to continue the work you've started.

Pump Primer 17: Letter-writing

When writing to someone, reread letters that others have sent you to recall what experiences, thoughts, and feelings are part of the sender's life. You may wish to prepare a filing system to keep together letters from the same friend. For each person you get a letter from, you may want to prepare a separate manila envelope. When an idea comes that you wish to include in a letter, jot it down. Don't worry about writing complete sentences. Just get the ideas down for later letter-writing. Each idea will be there as a pump primer for you when you write your next letter to that person. When you write to that person, recall experiences, thoughts, and feelings that have been part of his or her life.

Pump Primer 18: Phone Conversations

Tips for phone conversations are similar to those for writing letters. Here are some hints:

1. Make notes during phone conversations.

2. Store your notes in a manila envelope with the person's name on it.

3. Before calling the person, locate the manila envelope, pull out your notes, and refer to them.

Pump Primer 19: Initiate Reading with a Friend

For example, this is a helpful way you might begin reading this book, *Reminiscing Together*.

1. Talk with, call, or write to someone.

2. Agree upon a specific chapter you may each read at the same time.

3. As you read, make notes about times when you experienced what the chapter is talking about.

4. Tell your friend—by calling, face to face, or writing— about your thoughts.

5. This pump-primer activity works well for reading all sorts of material; magazine articles, newspaper articles. It could even be adapted to watching a particular TV program at the same time, then talking about it with your friend later.

Pump Primer 20: Finding Story-listeners

When seeking story-listeners, consider grandchildren and younger neighbors in your community. They may have more time to listen than some of the adults, including your own adult children. These young persons provide good opportunities to share your experiences—and can benefit from your experiences. It is very important to first talk with their parents to let them know of your interest in talking with the youngsters. When talking, ask the youngsters about what's going on in their lives. They may be particularly interested in learning what your life was like when you were their age. You have a lot to contribute to them, and at the same time you will learn what life is like for them.

Pump Primer 21: Helping Your Family to Listen

Lucille told us:

✦

The more experiences you have had, the more you have to share with others of all ages, particularly family members who may not have lived long enough to have the same kinds of experiences.

Our research has shown how the rich experiences of elders are helpful for younger persons. The best way to help other people listen to you is to first listen to them. Ask younger persons to help you by telling you stories of their experiences, contemporary issues, and life. Ask them, "What's on your mind that is important to you?" Then listen to their stories. Listen for when they ask, "Did anything like that happen to you?" Then it's your turn to share whatever you think of.

✦

1. Use photo albums or scrapbooks to arouse your family's interest in "what happened back then."

2. Let your family know that if they ask you for your story, it is important to you that they listen to you.

3. They can show their interest by not interrupting, and by asking open questions. (See "Taking Turns" in Chapter 1.)

WHAT YOU'D LIKE YOUR FAMILY TO KNOW ABOUT LISTENING

If you're a parent, you have spent a lot of time listening to your children's concerns. Now if you have children who are grown, it's important for you to tell them:

> I have concerns and now need equal time to share them with you, just as I listened to you when you were a child.

✦

We have to be honest enough to reveal our feelings and experiences as we tell our family of our concerns. This kind of honesty on the part of the parent evokes a sympathetic and listening ear from an adult child.

This sharing of feelings does wonders to create intimacy between family members. Don't be surprised if faces light up and hugs are exchanged!

About the Authors

The authors, Howard I. Thorsheim, Ph.D., and Bruce B. Roberts, Ph.D., who teach at St. Olaf College, Northfield, Minnesota, are internationally known researchers, authors, and lecturers in the field of psychology.

◆

Howard Thorsheim, professor of psychology at St. Olaf, holds a B.A. from St. Olaf, and an M.A. and Ph.D. from the University of Illinois at Champaign-Urbana. A "systems perspective" pervades all of his professional work. Dr. Thorsheim is a Licensed Consulting Psychologist, certified for competencies in systems ranging from physiological feedback mechanisms to social ecology. His research and teaching interests range from cognitive psycho-physiological investigations of knowledge representation to theoretical and applied study of the learning process, as well as to community work and the concept of "empowerment."

Dr. Thorsheim has taught several courses on learning and memory. Among his many other interests are youth and the prevention of youth alcohol and other drug abuse, and the impact of space development on social sciences and education.

He has been a presenter for professional organizations in this country, and in Canada, the British Isles, and Europe. In 1989, he and Bruce Roberts were invited to present a paper at the Fulbright International Colloquium on Communication, Health, and the Elderly at Gregynog, Wales.

Dr. Thorsheim's professional memberships include the American Psychological Association, the Cognitive Science Society, the Midwestern Psychological Association, the Gerontological Society of America, the American Institute of Aeronautics and Astronautics, the Psychonomic Society, the Human Factors Society, the American Association for Higher Education, and the International Society for the Systems Sciences.

✦

Bruce B. Roberts, Ph.D., professor of psychology and chair of St. Olaf's Department of Psychology, holds B.S. and M.Ed. degrees from Oregon State University and a Ph.D. from Claremont Graduate School and University Center.

Dr. Roberts has taught courses on the psychology of leadership and of counseling, and on social, environmental, and community psychology in the United States and in Norway.

He has contributed in important ways, as a researcher and author, in areas from community development and empowering leadership to substance abuse prevention. From 1980 to 1987, he was co-director, with Dr. Thorsheim, of the Social Ecology Research Project, initially created as part of a National Institute on Drug Abuse (NIDA) field research project.

Bruce Roberts and Howard Thorsheim have a long and productive academic partnership—as co-presenters for such groups as the American Psychological Association, the Midwest Psychological Association, and the International Society for General Systems Research (in Budapest, Hungary); as co-authors of several articles included in books and professional journals, and of a booklet developed during a NIDA research grant, *News About Booze* (800,000 copies were distributed to college freshmen by the National Collegiate Athletic Association); as co-designers and co-facilitators for such seminars as the Dakota LEADers Workshop on Empowering Leadership for Community Development (involving thirty-two communities in North and South Dakota), and five national workshops for youth leaders, sponsored jointly by American Lutheran Church, Lutheran Church in America, and Lutheran Church—Missouri Synod.

Much of the material and inspiration for *Reminiscing Together* paralleled the authors' study, "Elders As Consultants: The Lifestories Program," under the auspices of a grant from the Minnesota Private College Research Foundation funded by the Blandin Foundation of Park Rapids, Minnesota. Other sources of support and empowerment include: the United States Public Health Service (under what is now called U.S. Department of Health and Human Services), the Elderhostel Program, the Evangelical Lutheran Church in America, and the American Association of Retired Persons.

Drs. Thorsheim and Roberts live in Northfield with their families.

Appendix A

ACTION Ideas for Volunteering Skills and Experiences

RETIRED SENIOR VOLUNTEER PROGRAM (RSVP)

The Retired Senior Volunteer Program, a program of ACTION (the federal volunteer agency), recognizes the wealth of life experience and skills that elders have, and the resource these are for the community. The program also recognizes that it is healthy for our minds and spirits to be involved, to continue to contribute to our community. Typically RSVP volunteers contribute about four hours of service per week. What they do depends on each volunteer's interest and background. Many good ideas are suggested by this program. Among them are working with youth, consumer protection and support, in-home care (such as respite work), personal care, escorting, shopping, or working with support groups. Work might involve crime prevention, educational programs, fraud protection, self-defense, or neighborhood watches, for example.

FOSTER GRANDPARENT PROGRAM

The Foster Grandparent Program, another ACTION program, helps elders use their skills with children who have special needs. Men and women in the Foster Grandparent Program offer their experience and their willingness to share it. A brochure available from ACTION describes many useful ideas developed as part of the Foster Grandparent Program. The brochure contains personal statements about how important the program has been for participants. For example, Lennie Foster, 72, of Grand Junction, Colorado, says, "Being a Foster Grandparent is really fulfilling. I feel I've accomplished something when I help make life a little more worthwhile for someone."

SENIOR COMPANION PROGRAM (SCP)

In this ACTION program, Senior Companions are involved about twenty hours per week. Some of the ideas suggested by this program include:

- ✦ listening to others' life experiences;
- ✦ sharing your own life experiences;
- ✦ monitoring others' needs;
- ✦ household and personal care assistance (such as helping others exercise arms and legs);
- ✦ providing information about community services;
- ✦ helping them write letters to family members and friends;
- ✦ talking with them about current events so they can better understand our world;
- ✦ filling out forms;
- ✦ providing social and recreational support (such as walking with them across the room, around the block, or to the store).

Note in the materials you receive about this program that there are some special requirements plus pre- and in-service training as part of the preparation for elders who participate.

The tremendous involvement by elders in these programs is illustrated by the story of what has happened in the state of Minnesota. According to Tim Krieger of the Minnesota state office of ACTION, there are approximately 15,750 Minnesota elders involved in ACTION programs, which in 1989 alone provided over 2,100,000 hours of service to Minnesota communities!

In an evaluation conducted for ACTION, the benefit mentioned most—by 74 percent of elder volunteers who assist other adults with special needs—was "being able to help someone else." (Sociometrics, Inc. *An Evaluation of Family Caregiver Services.* Final Report Prepared for ACTION Program Analysis and Evaluation Division, Washington, D.C., December 1988; p. 31).

More information about any of these ACTION programs (the Retired Senior Volunteer Program, Foster Grandparent Program, or Senior Companion Program), and whom to contact in your area to learn more about them, is available from:

ACTION, The National Volunteer Agency
Office of Public Affairs
1100 Vermont Avenue NW
Washington, D.C. 20525
Telephone: 202/634-9108

So, there you have it! A way to enhance our lives is to assist others who need our help. That is the key. As we help others, we improve the quality of our lives. We have more to contribute and share. It works. Everybody benefits. This is worth *remembering* and *sharing* with others.

Appendix B

The American Association of Retired Persons (AARP) Reminiscence Program

The American Association of Retired Persons (AARP) Reminiscence Program, developed in 1983, utilizes the talents of older volunteers to give reminiscence training to families, friends, volunteer visitors, and professionals. Training materials include *The Reminiscence Training Guide,* as well as the brochure *Reminiscence: Finding Meaning in Memories.*

Benefits of the Reminiscence Program are summarized well by Kathryn Fowler, one of the AARP volunteers: "Reminiscence helps people build bridges of understanding across generations and between cultures. In reminiscing together, people, who might otherwise be strangers, see and enjoy their common humanity."

Reminiscence Program training has been used to develop a variety of other programs. These include visiting programs for homebound people and nursing home residents, library volunteer programs that combine delivery of books with reminiscence visiting. Contact AARP for several other ways to use reminiscing. For example, reminiscing may be part of high school volunteer programs in hospital settings, hospice programs, and programs for sharing memories and crafts.

Other related helpful resources available from AARP include brochures, such as:

> *Reminiscence: Reaching Back, Moving Forward* (a very helpful, brief summary of the benefits of reminiscing);
>
> *Now Where Did I Put My Keys?* (a self-help guide for understanding and improving memory);

So Many of My Friends Have Moved Away or Died (reflections and suggestions on making new friends);

If Only I Knew What to Say or Do (ideas for helping a friend in crisis);

I Wonder Who Else Can Help (questions and answers about counseling needs and resources).

For more information about these materials and how to become involved in the AARP reminiscence activities, contact:

American Association for Retired Persons (AARP)
Social Outreach and Support Section
1909 K Street NW
Washington, D.C. 20049
Telephone: 202/728-4370

Appendix C

Resources for Those with Visual Impairment

American Foundation for the Blind
15 West 16th Street
New York, New York 10011
Telephone: 800/232-5463

The American Foundation for the Blind (AFB) is a national nonprofit organization that advocates, develops, and provides programs and services to help blind and visually impaired people achieve independence with dignity in all sectors of society. Headquartered in New York City, AFB maintains regional centers in Atlanta,

Chicago, Dallas, San Francisco, New York City, and
Washington, D.C.

From AFB you may obtain a catalog called
AFB Products for Persons with Vision Problems.
This catalog describes games, educational
materials, and other resources to enhance
daily living activities.

> Fred Sammons, Inc.
> 145 Tower Drive
> P.O. Box 579
> Hinsdale, Illinois 60521
> Telephone: 800/323-5547

Fred Sammons, Inc., publishes the
Enrichments Catalog which pictures and
describes aids that make life easier for persons
with physical disabilities (including visual
impairments). Such aids include eating aids,
kitchen aids, aids for dressing and hygiene, shoe
aids, and communication aids.

The General Electric Company (GE) will provide
a service technician at no charge to put Braille
controls on GE electric ranges, certain microwave
ovens, and laundry equipment for consumers
with visual impairments.

> For more information, contact:

> GE Answering Service
> Telephone: 800/626-2000

(Braille services might be provided by other companies for a variety of products. Why not get together with friends to think of places in your home where Braille labels might be helpful? Together, think about whom you might contact to arrange Braille services.)

Appendix D

Resources for Those with Hearing Impairment

AT&T National Special Needs Center
2001 Route 46, Suite 310
Parsippany, New Jersey, 07054
Telephone: 800/233-1222 (Voice)
800/833-3232 (TDD/TTY)

The AT&T National Special Needs Center has aids and literature for the communicatively impaired person. The aids assist people with hearing, motion, and visual impairments. Adaptive aids include:

✦ TDDs (Telecommunication Devices for the Deaf) and TTYs (Tele-Typewriters);

✦ telecaption decoders (that "code" verbal telecaptions into a visual/sign language display);

✦ light switches that flash with incoming calls;

✦ Big Button Plus telephones;

✦ cordless phones;

✦ speaker phones that are activated by blowing into them (for people with motion impairment).

The people at AT&T encourage you to feel free to call them to discuss whatever aids you think you might need.

✦

SONIC ALERT
1750 West Hamlin Road
Rochester Hills, Michigan 48309
Telephone: 313/656-3110 (Voice and TDD)

SONIC ALERT offers catalogs that describe products to assist persons with hearing impairment.

Organizations

"SHHH" (Self Help for Hard of Hearing
    People)
7800 Wisconsin Avenue
Bethesda, Maryland 20814
Telephone: 301/657-2248 (Voice)
301/657-2249 (TDD)

"SHHH" is an international volunteer
organization of hearing-impaired people, their
relatives and friends. It is a nonprofit,
nonsectarian organization devoted to the
education, welfare, and interests of people with
hearing loss. The goal of "SHHH" is to assist
hearing-impaired people participate fully in the
hearing world. "SHHH" sponsors annual
conventions and a bimonthly *SHHH* magazine. It
has regional affiliates.

✦

The American Speech-Language-Hearing
    Association (ASHA)
10801 Rockville Pike
Rockville, Maryland 20852
Telephone: 301/897-5700 (Voice and TDD)
800/638-8255

ASHA is the national professional and
scientific association for speech-language

pathologists and audiologists concerned with communication behavior and disorders. ASHA provides informational brochures and packets on a broad range of speech-language and hearing disorders, including those that affect elders.

✦

The Alexander Graham Bell Association for
      the Deaf
3417 Volta Place NW
Washington, D.C. 20007
Telephone: 202/337-5220 (Voice and TDD)

This association provides information on speech reading, education, advocacy, aids and devices, and the social and psychological implications of deafness. The Oral Hearing Impaired Section (OHIS), an active service group of adults with hearing loss, offers special activities and programs for its members.

✦

The National Association of the Deaf
814 Thayer Avenue
Silver Spring, Maryland 20910
Telephone: 301/587-1788 (Voice and TDD)

The National Association of the Deaf provides information to anyone and their families about deafness, services to persons with deafness, communication skills, laws, employment rights, and advocacy.

◆

National Information Center on Deafness
    (NICD)
Gallaudet University
800 Florida Avenue NE
Washington, D.C., 20002
Telephone: 202/651-5000 (Voice and TDD)

The NICD provides information in all areas related to deafness. Services include education, vocational training, sign language programs, laws, technology, and barrier-free design. As needed, NICD makes referrals to local and community services. You may obtain a complete catalog of NICD's brochures by writing to the above address.

An example of the content of one of NICD's brochures is reprinted below with permission granted by the National Information Center on Deafness.

Communication Tips for Adults with Hearing Loss

by Harriet Kaplan, Ph.D., Assistant professor, Department of Audiology, Gallaudet College

"When you communicate, you share ideas, feelings, or information with at least one other person, usually by listening and speaking. If you have a hearing loss, however, speech may not be loud or clear enough, especially in a noisy or group situation. Words or sentences are misunderstood, and wrong messages are received. This often leads to embarrassment.

"Some people think that speechreading (watching the lips, facial expressions, and gestures of another person) can solve all these listening problems. Speechreading can be very helpful, because many words that are difficult to hear can be seen on the lips. But some communication situations remain difficult even when you use both your listening and speechreading skills together. Speechreading doesn't help much when the lighting is poor or when the speaker is too far away, doesn't move his/her lips, or covers his/her mouth. In most of these situations, listening is difficult as well.

"The group situation is particularly difficult for the hearing-impaired person. Keeping up with changing speakers presents problems; it's hard to listen to more than one person at one time or to keep up with the conversation when the topic changes suddenly. Even the best speechreader has problems with group communication.

"Other problems are caused by the nature of our language. Many sounds are not visible on the lips because they are made in the back of the mouth. Try saying the word cake while you watch yourself in the mirror. You won't see much movement. Watch yourself in the mirror while you say the following words: pat, bat, mat, pad, mad, bad. Can you see any difference?

"Adjustments are possible in difficult communication situations. First you must become aware of what is causing the communication breakdown. Then you can use positive strategies to improve your chances of receiving correct messages from the speaker. Let's discuss some of these strategies."

Coping with the Physical Setting

"You depend on your vision as well as your hearing to receive information. If you can't see the speaker clearly, you can't speechread very well. Perhaps the speaker is talking to you from another room or with his/her back turned. Perhaps the speaker is too far away. Here are some of the things you can do.

"A speaker who talks with his/her back to you or from another room probably does not understand the communication problem. It is your responsibility to explain to friends, relatives, and others in a tactful manner that you must see their faces clearly in order to understand. People who care will not be offended when you state your needs.

"If the speaker is in another room or too far away for comfortable conversation, move closer.

"If you are going to a meeting or a lecture, it is very important to have a seat close to the speaker so that you can speechread. This also helps listening. A good seat is located in the center of one of the front rows, away from pillars or supports. In order to get a good seat, you must arrive early. If this is not possible, perhaps someone will change seats with you. It is worth asking.

"If you can order theater tickets in advance, be sure to ask for a good seat. In order to do that, you must become familiar with the layout of the theater, order tickets early, and be willing to explain to the ticket agent why you need special seating.

"Use your vision well. If you suspect a visual problem, see your doctor. If you need to wear glasses, always use them when speechreading.

"At a meeting or a lecture, ask the presenter to use the blackboard or an overhead projector as much as possible. Also ask in advance for lecture notes or other written material about the lecture. Get a copy in advance of the agenda of a meeting you plan to attend. Knowing the topic or topics to be discussed helps considerably in understanding the spoken message.

"Arrange for someone to take notes for you at a meeting or lecture. That leaves you free to concentrate on listening and speechreading.

"Another way to keep up with discussion is to arrange for a flip-board to be used throughout the meeting. Topics of discussion and important information such as names and numbers are written on the flip-board as they come up. Arrange for the flip-board before the meeting.

"Proper seating is important for listening too, especially when you are using a hearing-aid. Avoid sitting near hard walls and other hard surfaces. Sound tends to bounce off such surfaces, creating distortion.

"Involve the speaker in improving the listening environment. Insist that he/she use a microphone at a meeting or lecture. If possible, discuss the use of the microphone with the speaker before the meeting. Sometimes, speakers are 'microphone shy' but will use one if asked. Keep in mind that other people also have problems when a speaker does not use a microphone. You are helping others as well as yourself.

"Another common problem with the physical setting is poor lighting. If the light is behind the speaker's back, you will see a face in a shadow and thus have trouble speechreading. The light should be directly overhead or slightly in front of the speaker (but not directed into your eyes). What are some things you can do in a situation with poor lighting?

"Tell your communication partner that you are having trouble speechreading because the lighting is poor. Show that person exactly how to change position so that you can see his or her face clearly. Most people will not be offended if you ask politely.

"At a lecture or meeting, discuss lighting problems with a presenter before the session starts. If you cannot plan in advance to avoid lighting problems, then choose a seat that allows the clearest view of the speaker.

"When you leave a dark place for a well-lit one, your eyes need a few minutes to adjust. Do not try to speechread during that time."

Managing Noisy Situations

"Hearing aids pick up all sound within range, noise as well as speech. At a party, in the cafeteria, or at home, noise can make communication almost impossible. What can you do?

"Let the speaker know you are having trouble hearing because of background noise. Suggest a quieter place to communicate. For example, if you are conversing next to a noisy fan, move to another part of the room. In a restaurant, sit at a table in a secluded corner.

"If possible, remove the source of noise. Sometimes we try to communicate with the television, radio, or running water turned on. These noises are easily eliminated.

"If possible, avoid rooms with poor acoustics. Rooms with hard walls, no carpeting, no acoustic tile on the ceiling, extensive window surfaces or no drapes make understanding difficult, even for people with normal hearing. If you go to meeting rooms frequently and have continual problems, ask that the meetings be transferred to a better place.

"There are special listening devices (induction loops, radio frequency hearing aids, or infrared systems) that can be installed in meeting rooms or auditoriums. These devices allow the speaker's voice to be made louder than competing noise. Ask your audiologist for information about such devices.

"Sometimes the noise in a room stops then starts, rather than continuing all the time. For example, if you are near an airport, airplane noise can make conversation very difficult. It is a good idea to stop conversation until the noise stops.

"Remember that communicating in noise is difficult for everyone, including normal hearing people. They make allowances for this and ask for help in noisy situations. You can, too."

Coping with a Poor Speaker

"We have all encountered people who speak with food, a cigarette, or a pipe in their mouths. People with normal hearing have problems understanding such individuals, but communication becomes even more difficult when the listener has a hearing loss. Other speaker characteristics may not prove very difficult for the hearing person, but may complicate communication for the hearing impaired. These include the speaker who talks too fast and uses distracting gestures, limited facial expression, or little mouth movement. In addition, a beard or mustache that covers the lips often makes speechreading difficult. What can be done?

"Explain the difficulty to the speaker and indicate tactfully what you need for better communication. Explain that it is impossible to speechread individuals with things in or covering their mouths. In most cases, the speaker is probably not aware that these habits are interfering with speech understanding.

"Ask the person to speak a little more slowly. A slow rate of speech often has other benefits. Distracting head movements then tend to slow down or even stop. Words are pronounced more clearly. Sometimes a person also uses more facial expression and clearer mouth movements when speaking more slowly. Sometimes the speaker will also talk a little louder.

"If the speaker is a friend or a relative, feel free to ask that the mustache or beard be trimmed to make lips more visible. Often the person will be glad to do so. If not, nothing has been lost.

"Remember that time can contribute to improved communication. Sometimes it is possible to become accustomed to a particular pattern of speech. The more you talk with a person, the easier it becomes to understand, even if that person has poor speech habits."

Managing the Group Situation

"Understanding conversation in a group is probably the most difficult communication situation for a hearing-impaired person. One problem is that the conversation may jump quickly from person to person. By the time you identify the new speaker, some of the message is lost. In addition, some of the speakers may not be visible to you because of your physical position. This is a common situation when you are part of an audience and a person in back of you asks a question.

"Still another problem relates to the topic of conversation. If you enter a group in the middle of a discussion, you will probably not know the topic. Normal-hearing people face the same problem of catching up with the conversation, but this task is far more difficult when a person cannot hear clearly. A sudden change of topic usually leaves the hearing-impaired person totally lost. Although a shift of topic may occur in one-to-one communication, it is far more difficult to get on the right track in a group. Here are some strategies that can help:

"When the conversation shifts rapidly from person to person, a speaker can signal in some way before starting to talk. You can ask the speakers to raise a finger or a hand before talking. This strategy can work well at the dinner table or in a group discussion.

"In group situations, some hearing-impaired people use a microphone attached to their hearing aids by a long cable. The microphone is passed from speaker to speaker as needed. This arrangement not only makes the speaker's voice louder but also identifies the person who is talking.

"To help when the topic of conversation changes, a friend or relative can serve as a 'cuer' to tell you when and to what the topic has changed. You need to tell everyone else of this arrangement and ask for a short delay in the conversation while your 'cuer' tells you of the new topic. At a meeting you could ask the group leader to indicate in some way when the topic changes. Perhaps the leader can interject at the proper moment 'We are now talking about...'

"If you enter a situation in which a conversation is already in progress, always ask, 'What are we talking about?' or something similar.

"If several people are talking at one time, tell the group you can understand only one person at a time. Many normal-hearing people have the same problem.

"In order to see the maximum number of people in a group, seat yourself appropriately. The best position will vary with the situation. In order to see the maximum number of people at a table, it is best to sit at the head or foot rather than the side. You can see more people without having to move your body.

In a living room, it is better to sit on a chair than a sofa. People sitting next to you on the sofa are difficult to see, making it necessary to speechread from the side rather than the front.

"If you are at a lecture or a large meeting and cannot see a person speaking from the audience, wait until the person is finished. Then raise your hand and ask the group leader to repeat the question or comment. Even better, arrange this with the group leader in advance. Used tactfully, this strategy will not disrupt the proceedings. Another approach is to ask the questioner to stand up and repeat what he said."

When You Don't Understand Something

"Sometimes, in spite of all your efforts, you simply don't understand what a person is saying. The strategy that most people use is repetition. If you don't understand the repetition, however, it is not a good idea to ask the speaker to say something a third time. There are other ways to clarify a misunderstood message:

"You can repeat back the part of the sentence that was understood and ask the speaker to supply the rest. For example, the speaker might say, 'I met John in the store.' Your problem is that you didn't catch the name. You might say, 'You met who at the store?' The speaker them knows specifically how to help.

"You can ask for clarification of what the speaker said. For example, if you do not understand directions, you might say, 'I think you told me to turn right at the next corner. Is that correct?' Another approach is to ask, 'Did you say right at the next corner?'

"The speaker may be asked to rephrase a statement that you did not understand. You can say, 'I'm sorry, I don't understand. Can you say it another way?'

"If you do not understand a specific word, such as a name or a number, you can ask the speaker to spell or write it. This is useful if you must have precise information. If the speaker spells a word and you do not understand the spoken letters, it is possible to use a code word to clarify the spelling. You can ask, 'Was that "A" as in apple?'

"If you are having trouble understanding a spoken number, you can ask the speaker to give the number one digit at a time. For example, one hundred forty-four can be spoken as one-four-four. Each spoken digit can be reinforced by showing the appropriate number of fingers. Speaking numbers as individual digits can be helpful with telephone communication as well as face-to-face conversation.

"Another useful strategy for small numbers is counting. If you cannot understand a number, you can ask the speaker to count from zero and stop at the correct number. You can even silently count along with the speaker to be sure that you have the correct number. This strategy is very useful on the telephone.

"A combination of these two strategies will work as well for large numbers. There are several ways for a speaker to say numbers. The number 2,454, for example, can be 'two thousand four hundred fifty-four,' or 'twenty-four fifty-four.' If you understand neither, ask the speaker to count up to each number in sequence: 'one-two'; 'one-two-three-four'; 'one-two-three-four-five'; 'one-two-three-four.'

"Practice these strategies whenever appropriate. You will find they make communication easier both for you and your communication partner."

Some Other Tactics

"Be interested and interesting. Current events are often the topic of conversation, so be aware of what is happening nationally and locally. Keep up with sports news, with popular TV shows, with what is happening in your neighborhood. Keep up with your friends' interests. Develop your own interests and hobbies and share them with your friends. By doing these things, you will be better prepared to understand most conversations. In addition, other people will want to talk with you and make an extra effort to help you communicate.

"Be prepared. When you go to a movie or play, read the reviews or summary of the plot in advance. You will have a better idea of what is being said and will enjoy the performance more. Prepare for meetings by getting prior information about topics and agenda so that you can practice recognizing important words. Also, you will be ready for topic changes. Before you go into a particular situation, think of what a speaker is likely to say. Make a list of vocabulary appropriate to that situation and practice recognizing those words. For example, you can predict pretty well what the garage mechanic will say when you take your car in for service.

"Be observant. Watch everything about the speaker. Watch the facial expressions and body language. Most people will raise their eyebrows when asking a question and shake their heads to indicate a negative statement. You can often tell when someone is angry from the facial expressions and body position. If a speaker is talking about a particular person, he/she may point to or look at that person. All of this is valuable information.

"**Be honest and assertive.** Do not pretend to understand when you are confused. The speaker usually notices this after a while and may feel that you are not interested in the conversation. The speaker may also wonder about your intelligence. It is much better to identify your hearing loss to other people and admit when you don't understand. Most people will try to help if you tell them what to do. The assertive person admits the problem and pleasantly tells the speaker exactly what kind of help is needed to improve communication.

"**Keep your sense of humor.** Even when you make a mistake and feel foolish, your willingness to laugh at yourself will help everyone to relax and feel comfortable."

Conclusions

"The suggested strategies can aid communication in various situations. You may feel comfortable using some, while others may not be useful to you. Perhaps you have developed additional ways of coping not discussed here. Any strategy that works for you is fine. Experiment with the techniques discussed in this fact sheet and others you can think of. Use what you find helpful.

"Regardless of which strategies you choose, the important things to remember are:

"Be honest with your hearing loss.

"Be assertive about asking for help.

"Always think about how you can keep communication going."

Note: Special permission was obtained to reprint this brochure, *Communication Tips for Adults with Hearing Loss,* in this book. For price information on additional copies of this publication, contact the National Information Center on Deafness.

National Information Center on Deafness, Gallaudet College, 800 Florida Avenue NE, Washington, DC 20002, (202) 651-5109 (Voice), (202) 651-5976 (TDD).

Series Editor: Loraine DiPietro, director, National Information on Deafness, Gallaudet College

Suggested Readings

Bower, S.A., and G.G. Bower. *Asserting Yourself, A Practical Guide for Positive Change.* Reading, Mass.: Addison-Wesley, 1976.

142 ✦

Castle, D. Telephone training for the deaf. *Volt Review*, 1977, 79, 373-378.

Harrelson, L.M. Strategies for the hearing impaired. *Hearing Instruments*, October 1982, 33(10), 9-10.

Jacobs, M. *Speechreading Strategies.* Rochester, N.Y.: National Technical Institute for the Deaf, 1979.

Nithart, T. Some practical approaches to hearing rehabilitation. *Hearing Instruments*, October 1982, 33(10), 14-15.

Pappas, J.J., G.S. Grahm, and C.R. Rols. Psychological problems associated with hearing impairment. *Hearing Instruments*, October 1982, 33(10), 22-23.

Rupp, R.R. and A.Z. Heavenrich. Positive communicative game rules:

> Part 1. *Hearing Instruments*, September 1982. 33(9), 34.

> Part 2. *Hearing Instruments*, October 1982, 33(10), 16-19

> Part 3. *Hearing Instruments*, November 1982, 33(11), 20-22.

LET US HEAR YOUR IDEAS

If you would like to share how one of the Pump Primer ideas was particularly helpful to you—or you would like to share a Pump Primer that you have found helpful—please drop us a line or call about it, and perhaps we can include it in the next edition!

> Howard I. Thorsheim, Ph.D.
> Bruce B. Roberts, Ph.D.
> St. Olaf College
> Northfield, Minnesota 55057
> Telephone: 507/663-3142